SYMBOLS OF AMERICAN FREEDOM

The White House

Farmington Public Library

by Mari Schuh

BLASTOFF! READERS

BELLWETHER MEDIA • MINNEAPOLIS, MN

Note to Librarians, Teachers, and Parents:

Blastoff! Readers are carefully developed by literacy experts and combine standards-based content with developmentally appropriate text.

Level 1 provides the most support through repetition of high-frequency words, light text, predictable sentence patterns, and strong visual support.

Level 2 offers early readers a bit more challenge through varied simple sentences, increased text load, and less repetition of high-frequency words.

Level 3 advances early-fluent readers toward fluency through increased text and concept load, less reliance on visuals, longer sentences, and more literary language.

Level 4 builds reading stamina by providing more text per page, increased use of punctuation, greater variation in sentence patterns, and increasingly challenging vocabulary.

Level 5 encourages children to move from "learning to read" to "reading to learn" by providing even more text, varied writing styles, and less familiar topics.

Whichever book is right for your reader, Blastoff! Readers are the perfect books to build confidence and encourage a love of reading that will last a lifetime!

This edition first published in 2019 by Bellwether Media, Inc.

No part of this publication may be reproduced in whole or in part without written permission of the publisher. For information regarding permission, write to Bellwether Media, Inc., Attention: Permissions Department, 6012 Blue Circle Drive, Minnetonka, MN 55343.

Library of Congress Cataloging-in-Publication Data

Names: Schuh, Mari C., 1975- author.
Title: The White House / by Mari Schuh.
Description: Minneapolis, MN : Bellwether Media, Inc., 2019. | Series: Blastoff! Readers: Symbols of American Freedom | Includes bibliographical references and index.
Identifiers: LCCN 2017061652 (print) | LCCN 2017061740 (ebook) | ISBN 9781626178908 (hardcover : alk. paper) | ISBN 9781618914767 (pbk. : alk. paper) | ISBN 9781681035536 (ebook)
Subjects: LCSH: White House (Washington, D.C.)–Juvenile literature. | Presidents–United States–Juvenile literature. | Washington (D.C.)–Buildings, structures, etc.–Juvenile literature.
Classification: LCC F204.W5 (ebook) | LCC F204.W5 S38 2019 (print) | DDC 975.3–dc23
LC record available at https://lccn.loc.gov/2017061652

Editor: Rebecca Sabelko   Designer: Andrea Schneider

Printed in the United States of America, North Mankato, MN.

Table of
Contents

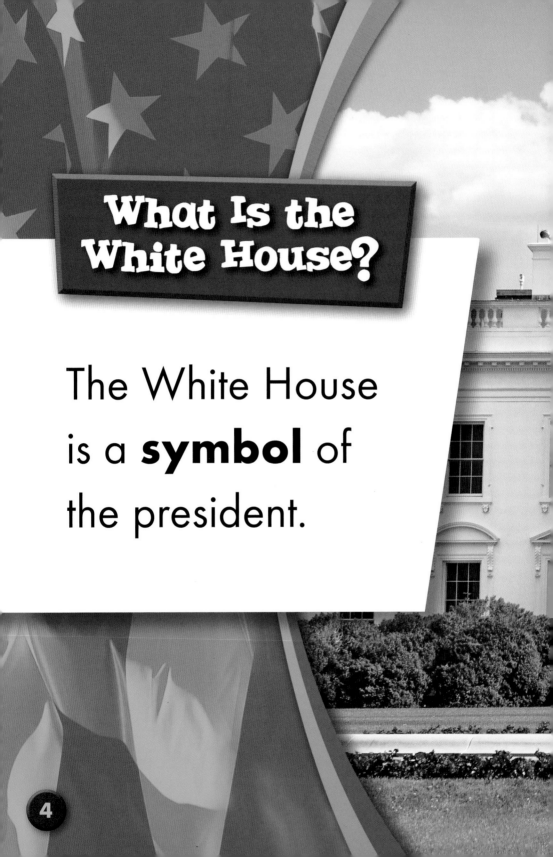

What Is the White House?

The White House is a **symbol** of the president.

It also stands for **democracy**. It is in Washington, D.C.

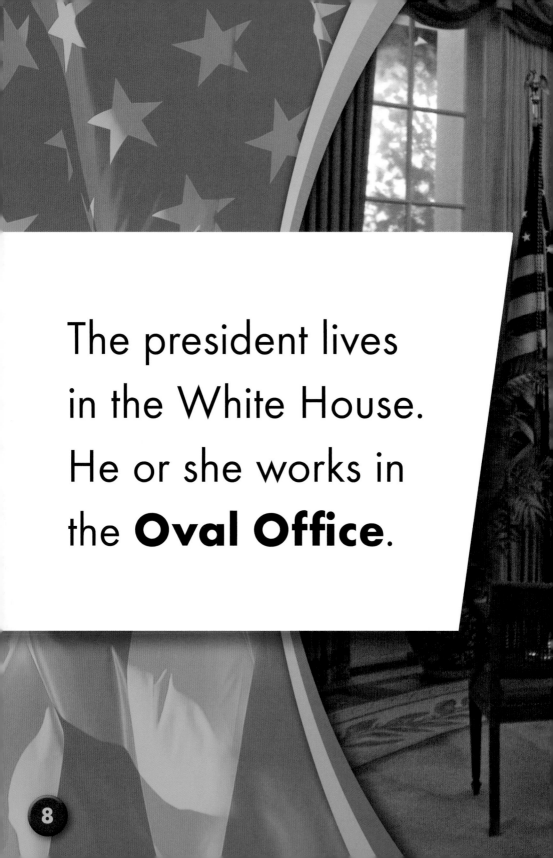

The president lives in the White House. He or she works in the **Oval Office**.

Parts of the
White House

East Wing

West Wing

Oval Office

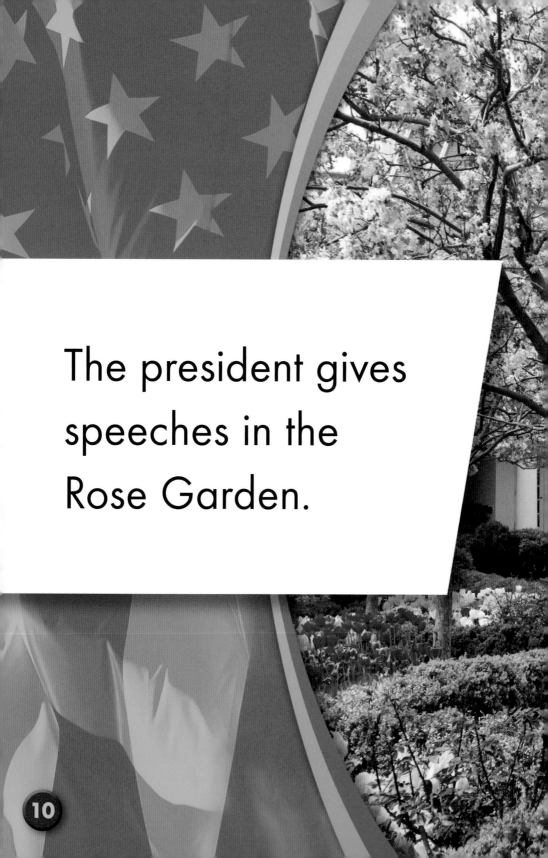

The president gives speeches in the Rose Garden.

A Historic House

Since 1800, the White House is where important decisions have been made.

World leaders meet
with the president
at the White House.
They sign **treaties**.

President Roosevelt signing trade treaty

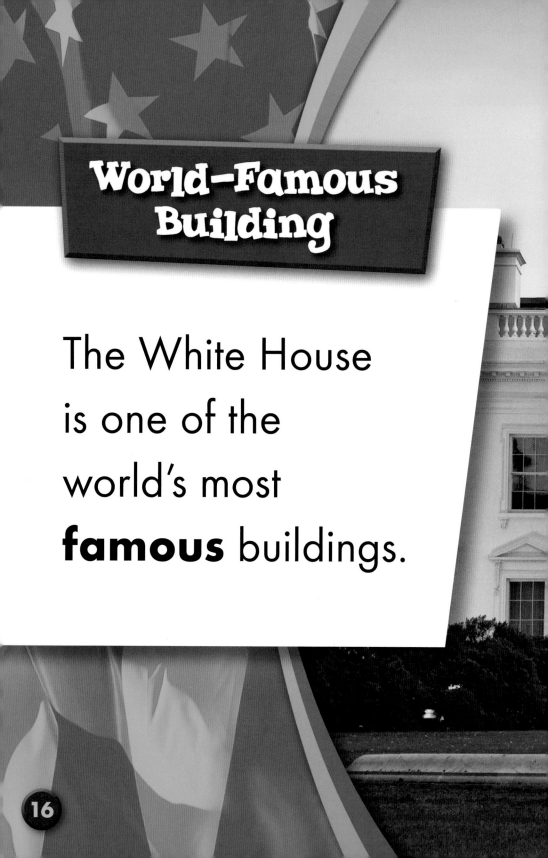

World-Famous Building

The White House is one of the world's most **famous** buildings.

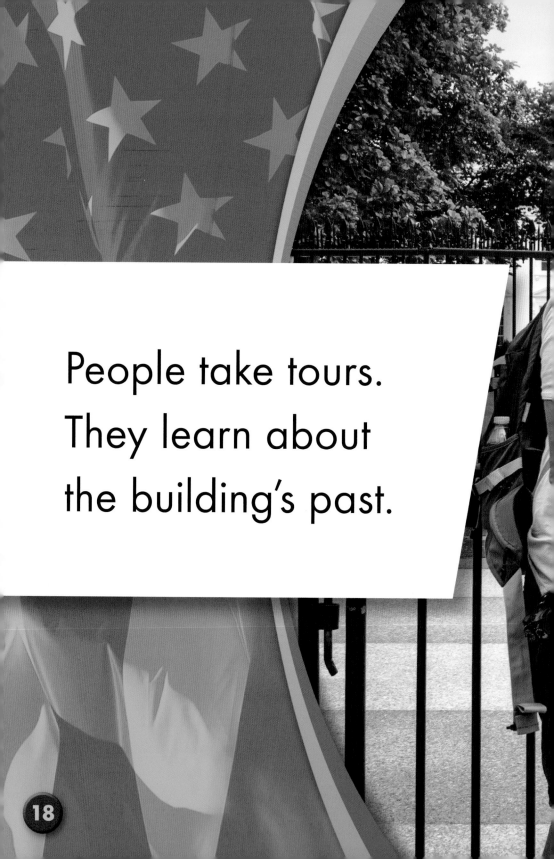

People take tours.
They learn about
the building's past.

18

The White House is part of U.S. history. It is a symbol of America!

Glossary

democracy

a government in which the people choose their leaders

symbol

something that stands for something else

famous

very well-known

treaties

agreements between two or more countries or governments

Oval Office

the president's office in the White House

To Learn More

AT THE LIBRARY

Bailey, R.J. *White House*. Minneapolis, Minn.: Bullfrog Books, 2017.

Murray, Julie. *The White House*. Minneapolis, Minn.: Abdo Kids, 2017.

Sipperley, Keli. *The White House*. Vero Beach, Fla.: Rourke Educational Media, 2015.

ON THE WEB

Learning more about the White House is as easy as 1, 2, 3.

1. Go to www.factsurfer.com.

2. Enter "White House" into the search box.

3. Click the "Surf" button and you will see a list of related web sites.

With factsurfer.com, finding more information is just a click away.

Index

The images in this book are reproduced through the courtesy of: turtix, front cover; By Honey Maple, p. 3; Orhan Camp, pp. 4-5; Rob Wilson, pp. 6-7; Chuck Aghoian, pp. 9, 10, 22 (bottom left); Valentina Breschi AFP/ Newscom, pp. 8-9; TriggerPhoto, pp. 10-11; North Wind Picture Archive/ Alamy, pp. 12-13; Harris & Ewing/ Wiki Commons, pp. 14-15; Richard Nowitz, pp. 16-17; BlackMac, pp. 18-19; Chris Parypa Photography, pp. 20-21; Yuganov Konstanti, p. 22 (middle left); 279photo Studio, p. 22 (middle right); vchal, p. 22 (top left); Monkey Business Images, p. 22 (top right).